A WALK THROUGH
THE
BIBLE

A WALK THROUGH
THE
BIBLE

Lesslie Newbigin

TRIANGLE

First published in Great Britain in 1999 by
Triangle
Society for Promoting Christian Knowledge
Holy Trinity Church
Marylebone Road
London NW1 4DU

Second Impression 2000

British Library Cataloguing-in-Publication Data

A catalogue record for this book is available from
the British Library

ISBN 0-281-05253-0

Typeset by Pioneer Associates, Perthshire
Printed in Great Britain by
Omnia Books Limited, Glasgow

Contents

The Newbigin family and the publishers
would like to thank Madeleine Bedford,
who originally suggested to
Lesslie Newbigin that he broadcast
a series of talks on the story of the
whole Bible (published here for the
first time) and produced the series
for Premier Radio.

Foreword

I first met Bishop Lesslie Newbigin when he came one evening to a concert in Holy Trinity Brompton, which was being given by the New English Orchestra. Someone pointed him out to me and I went over to introduce myself. I took the opportunity to ask somewhat diffidently if he would ever be willing to find time to come and talk to us as a church. He instantly and very graciously agreed. In this way started an association over several years which was of enormous benefit to us and which led to a warmth and friendship with me and the church that he was kind enough to express both publicly and privately until his death. I think he loved the opportunity to teach; he loved life and he loved the young.

Church life, as I'm sure many will readily agree, is often marked by extraordinary highs and profound lows. Occasionally there comes a mountain top moment which seems to rekindle faith, restore vision and revive our missionary zeal. One such moment in the life of our church was Lesslie Newbigin's tutoring at our annual church teaching holiday in July 1997. Of course we had many high moments with him as he taught in our Bible School with an astonishing range of learning and compassion and an extraordinary eagerness for the flourishing of Christ's church. On this occasion, which sadly proved to be his last at the school, he stood and without notes over two mornings told the story of the Bible. You can read what he said in this book.

It is difficult to describe the effect of these two hours. It was as if the whole of his life and ministry were summed up in the telling of this story. After all the years of outstanding scholarship and missionary endeavour he had come back to this – the great narrative of the Bible. As the Victorian hymn writer Arabella C. Hankey put it:

> Tell me the old, old story
> Of unseen things above,
> of Jesus and His glory
> Of Jesus and His love.
> Tell me simply, as to a little child,
> For I am weak and weary,
> And helpless and defiled.

Lesslie told us the old, old story simply but with remarkable power. It is of course the story he had come to see is true above all other stories. It is the only story through which humanity and history can be understood. It is the only story that, in its ending foreshadowed in Christ's resurrection, holds out hope for the world. It is the story in which he lived and that had shaped him. It is the story he handled with consummate skill in bringing it to bear on every aspect of not only church life, but also the wider culture of the world. One might say that Bishop Lesslie's passion was to see this story kept alive so that in the face of increasing secularization it, and in particular its Hero, might come once again to be the key determinant in shaping us and the societies in which we find ourselves. 'Here it is,' he seemed to be saying, 'guard it, live it, proclaim it.'

At his funeral service his son told of the habit Lesslie had developed of composing little limericks when he couldn't sleep at night! One such seemed so typical of him:

> There once was a man of Turin
> Who could preach several hours about sin,
> But, as he never left space to talk about grace,
> He never got under my skin.

Lesslie was the opposite. He talked constantly about the grace and love of God.

At his memorial service at Southwark Cathedral a prayer was prayed that gave thanks for his life but, more than that, expressed our desire for strength to carry on the work of proclaiming Jesus he had left off. Here it is:

Almighty God, Father of the heavenly lights,
Who does not change like shifting shadows,
We thank you for the life of Lesslie Newbigin
Which we celebrate as your good gift to us.
For the breadth of his vision,
For the depth of his thinking,
For the strength of his friendship,
For the laughter in his heart,
For his faithfulness in following Jesus,
We give you thanks.
And, in the knowledge that he is safe
with you,
And dwells at last in the habitations of
your glory,
Move us, by his example, to take up afresh
The unfinished agenda.
For Jesus Christ's sake,
Amen.

What a fitting memorial to him that would be and my hope is that this book will inspire many to do just that. I can't think of anything he would have liked more!

Sandy Millar
Vicar, Holy Trinity Brompton

A unique account

FOR at least a thousand years, the Bible was, for practical purposes, the only book known to people in Europe. They didn't have it in their hands before the days of printing, of course. They knew it through the teaching of the Church: through its readings, its preaching, its liturgy and sacraments; through the cycles of the seasons of the Christian year; through art, music and architecture.

The story told by the Bible was *the* story by which people understood the meaning of their lives, and for several centuries, even after the invention of printing in Europe in the mid fifteenth century, it was the only book most households had. Most households today have a Bible. But do people read it in the way they read other books? Do they read it as a whole, as a story from beginning to end? I think not. Most of us treat the Bible as an anthology of helpful thoughts to which we may occasionally turn, and from which we can obtain comfort, guidance, direction. And even in our readings of the Bible in church, we tend to look at only very short passages which reinforces the impression that the Bible is a collection of nuggets of wisdom from which we can choose what we find helpful. But in that case, of course, it is not the Bible itself that decides what is worth reading: we decide in advance. The Bible is not our authority.

Many years ago a Hindu friend of mine, a very learned man, said to me something I have never forgotten:

'I can't understand why you missionaries present the Bible to us in India as a book of religion. It is not a book of religion – and anyway we have plenty of books of religion in India. We don't need any more! I find in your Bible a unique interpretation of universal history, the history of the whole of creation and the history of the human race. And therefore a unique interpretation of the human person as a responsible actor in history. That is unique. There is nothing else in the whole religious literature of the world to put alongside it.'

He was right. And when he said the Bible is not a book of religion, what he meant was that it is not a book which encourages us to turn away from the down-to-earth business of ordinary life, from our responsibilities as actors in history. It does not encourage us to turn away from the world of our daily newspapers to a so-called spiritual world beyond. It is rather an interpretation of the whole of history from the creation to its end, and of the human story within that creation. And that is the story I want to tell.

Before we begin let me say three things about this story. The first thing is that every good story has a hero or heroine. The Bible has a hero and that hero is God, because the Bible interprets the whole of reality and the whole of history in terms of the actions, the doings, the speakings, the promises of God. And therefore the Bible is the way in which we come to know God, because we don't know a person except by knowing his or her story.

The second point is that the Bible tells the story of the whole human race in terms of a particular story of one race – that of Israel – and of one person within that race – Jesus of Nazareth. It doesn't directly tell us the story of China or Mexico. The story of all the nations is the background of the biblical story, as we shall see – but it is not at the centre.

The story is told from the point of view of the

people whom God chose to be the bearers of his purpose, because God does not wish to make himself known to us in the isolation of our own individual souls. He doesn't communicate with us on a one-to-one basis as if by telephone. God makes himself known to us in the context of our shared life as human beings because that is what our human life is. We therefore come to know God through one another – and specifically through the people whom he chose to be the bearers of his purpose.

Thirdly, to be those chosen people, to be the place where God is made known in history, is to be chosen for suffering, for agony, for conflict – and that is the story that the Bible tells.

IN THE BEGINNING . . .

And now let us turn to look at this book, and let us look at those majestic words with which the Bible opens:

> In the beginning God created the heavens and the earth.

This first chapter of Genesis was almost certainly written during the time when Israel was in exile in Babylon. And we must picture these writers as slaves under the shadow of this mighty empire with its palaces, fortresses and temples. Babylon had its own account of creation, as we know from the work of modern scholarship. It was a story of conflict, battle and bloodshed. Violence was the theme underlying the whole creation story as the Babylonians understood it.

The writers of Genesis had a quite different picture of God. They were the descendants of Abraham, Isaac, Jacob and Moses. They knew God as the redeemer God, the God who had saved his people from bondage. And they had a totally different picture of God's creation – not as the result of violence but as the action of a God of love and wisdom who, out of sheer love, desired to create a world to reflect his glory and a human family to enjoy his world and give back his love.

And so we have in Genesis a picture of the creation of light to be distinguished from darkness, of the dry land to be distinguished from the chaos of the sea, of a home in which living creatures could grow and thrive, of the creation of the animals and of human beings among them, and of the special responsibility given to human beings of being in the image of God.

And to this human family he has given the specific responsibility of cherishing his creation, of bringing it to that perfection for which God intended it, so that it, with the whole human race, should truly reflect his glory.

And finally, as the climax of the story we have this wonderful picture of God resting on the sabbath day to enjoy his works, to look at his creation and enjoy it, and his gift to us human beings of that same rest, so that our life is not a ceaseless struggle but at the heart of it there is this invitation simply to rest and enjoy God. Joy is that for which the world was made. In the great words of the Scottish Catechism:

The purpose for which we were made is to glorify God and enjoy him for ever.

But as we know it is not like that now. What has gone wrong? Here we come to the Bible's unique insight. The thing we don't like to talk about. The thing that New Age spirituality tries to hide. The thing theologians call 'the Fall'. What has happened? We have been given freedom. And we have been given knowledge of the goodness of God. God did not want us to know evil; he wanted us to know only good. But there creeps in that little snake of suspicion: 'Should we not find out for ourselves the other side of the picture? There must be another side. Why should it be hidden from us? We are free, we are responsible, is it not our duty to find out all the facts? Let us find out for ourselves what is good and what is evil. Surely we can't simply trust God for that!'

And so the fatal step is taken, the bond of trust is broken, and we are lost. We know that we are naked, vulnerable, easily hurt. We hide ourselves from God. We compete with each other. The neighbour given to us to be a neighbour becomes our rival. The world given to us to be our garden becomes a wilderness with which we have to fight.

And so there comes that terrible cry echoing throughout the garden:

'Adam, where are you?'

It is the cry of a mother whose child has run away in a crowded supermarket, a cry of anguish, a mixture of wrath and love; it's a cry that echoes right through the Bible as this loving and holy God seeks the children, the foolish stupid unbelieving children, who have run away because they thought they could find out for themselves better than God could tell them.

And right through the Bible runs the anguish of God as he seeks his foolish people. And it finally is echoed in that terrible cry from the cross when the son of God puts himself in the place of the rebellious Adam, in our place who have run away from God, and he cries out in anguish:

'My God, my God, why hast thou forsaken me?'

God will not leave us until he has won us back to be his children.

Chosen by God

WE have come to the point where Adam and Eve decided that they could not trust God but must find out for themselves what is good and what is evil. That act of mistrust brought to an end the innocent relationship with God, with one another and with the natural world.

BECAUSE now we have to depend upon ourselves to decide what is good and what is wrong, and because we know we are not capable of this, we are anxious, and because we are anxious, we become aggressive. Our neighbour becomes our rival, the natural world is no longer our home but a hostile environment to be tamed. There is a descent into violence. And the story is told with terrible clarity in the following chapters of Genesis. The first two brothers, Cain and Abel, become respectively murderer and victim. Murder, jealousy, strife, become the order of the day, and the whole human world degenerates into chaos in a spiral of violence.

NOAH IS CHOSEN

And so the point comes when God is sorry that he started the experiment. He decides to wipe the earth clean of this evil race, keeping only one family to make a fresh start – the family of Noah. And when that family comes out of the ark on to land which is once again dry, God makes a gracious covenant with Noah – and not only with Noah but with the whole creation – promising that never again will he destroy the earth, promising that Noah's descendants will fill the world and replenish it with happy people, and providing in the rainbow a sign of his promise.

And so in the next chapter (Genesis 10) we have the beginning of the fulfilment of that promise: the seventy nations into which the Hebrew people divided the human world are described as the descendants of Noah. They are what in the rest of the Bible are called the Gentiles or the heathen; they are the background of the whole story. They are introduced to us here as the result of God's promise to Noah, and throughout the Bible they are the ultimate recipients of God's blessing. But once again the same sad story is repeated. The nations who are spread over the earth are no longer content to have what one might call a human's eye view of the world. Once again they want a God's eye view.

> 'Let us build a tower with its top in heaven so that we can really see the whole scene from above and not just from below.'

And so there is the tower of Babel, or Babylon – symbol of all the great imperial powers that have sought to unify people on the basis of a human programme.

ABRAHAM IS CHOSEN

But once again the end is disaster. The human race is scattered in mutual incomprehension around the world. And once again the patient God makes another fresh start. From among these heathen nations he chooses one man, a wealthy man, with many flocks and herds and servants, living in one of the great centres of power and civilization of the ancient world – Ur of the Chaldeans. And God calls this man to leave his home, his wealth, his security, and to go to a land which he does not know, trusting only in the promise of God.

Here is the beginning of a new kind of human living, one that does not depend on the securities we have accumulated over the past, but depends wholly on what God has promised for the future. A new kind of life – living by faith. And so Abraham makes his journey into the land of Canaan, and with his son Isaac and his grandson Jacob they live there as strangers in a foreign land – a land which has been promised to them and yet in which they possess nothing except a grave in which to bury their dead.

But even here, these people called to the life of faith are once again subject to grave trial. Famine drives them into Egypt where they become first of all refugees and then slaves, oppressed, downtrodden by the most powerful military regime in the known world. Eventually they become so numerous that their oppressors call for population control. The male Israelites are to be slaughtered. One of them escapes: Moses is rescued by a daughter of Pharaoh, and brought up in the imperial court.

MOSES IS CHOSEN

As a young man Moses becomes an heir to the riches, the learning, the culture, the science, the technology of the greatest civilizing power in the world at that time. And yet he knows at the same time that these slaves are his kinsmen. One day in a fit of fury, seeing an Egyptian beating one of his fellow Israelites, he loses his temper and kills the Egyptian, and then when his sin is discovered, flees, and takes refuge as a double refugee among the tribe of Canaanites in the Sinai peninsula.

There he marries his employer's daughter and settles down to the life of a shepherd. But God has not forgotten his promise. One day as Moses is out with his flocks in the shimmering heat of the desert he sees a bush burning and yet not being consumed. And coming near to see what is going on he hears himself addressed:

'Moses, Moses.'
'Yes?'
'I am sending you to rescue my people from Egypt.'
'Who me? You must be joking! A fleeing rebel? Who am I to rescue your people?'
'But I will be with you.'
'But who are you? If I go to the Israelites and say, "Someone, I don't know who, has sent me to rescue you", won't they ask me who he is?

17

What is his name? What is your name?'
'"I will be who I will be." That is my name.
"Yahweh." "Jehovah." "The Lord." Your ances-
tors knew me by the name that all Semites
know for God, "Allah", "El", but they did not
know my personal name. This is my name. I
will be with you.'

THE PEOPLE ARE CHOSEN

And so Moses goes, and there is that mighty
struggle with the power of Egypt which the
book of Exodus tells, and finally Moses leads his
people out of Egypt across the Red Sea and into
the desert of Sinai. A rabble of slaves. And what
a rabble. At every sign of trouble their hearts
melt. When they have no water they want to kill
Moses. When they have no food they want to
turn back again to Egypt where at least they had
something to eat. But Moses, endlessly patient
with them, struggles with their follies and finally
brings them as God had commanded to that
same mountain where God had promised to
meet them. And there God makes a covenant
with them to be a royal priesthood and a holy
nation.

Note first of all that it is a covenant not a

contract, it is not something mutually agreed as the result of bargaining. It is a unilateral action on the part of the sovereign Lord who has taken this rabble of slaves to be his people and committed himself absolutely to them, to be faithful to them even when they are unfaithful to him. And they are to be a priesthood to all the nations; through them the righteousness of God is to be revealed. And so God gives to them those famous ten words – what we call the ten commandments.

And it is very important to recognize two things about these ten commandments. People often criticize them for being negative, but the first great statement is not negative but positive:

'I am the Lord your God who brought you out of the land of Egypt. I am the one who rescued you, so don't go after other gods.'

We are tempted to follow all kinds of gods who promise all kinds of good things: prosperity, pleasure, happiness and everything:

'But they don't really love you. I am the God who loves you, and who rescued you and who brought you out of the land of Egypt. So don't go after other gods.'

That is a tremendously positive statement. And then there are some negatives: don't commit adultery, don't murder, don't steal, don't covet, etc. But you see the great point about a negative command is that it leaves you free. Positive commandments telling you exactly what to do in every situation don't leave you any freedom. A negative commandment leaves you freedom within limits. It's like the fence around a school playground. It leaves the children inside absolutely free to develop their own games, to do their own thing, but they know that outside the fence there is danger. And Israel through all its generations never ceased to thank God for the fact that they had been given that fence. As compared with the other nations of the world, who did not have that protection, and who were constantly tempted to stray away into all kinds of follies, leading to lying and adultery and murder and corruptions of all kinds, the people of Israel were grateful that they had been given this protection. All through their history there is a continual thanksgiving to God for this wonderful gift.

20

And so God calls Israel to be a holy priesthood for all the nations, to be the nation through whom the rest of the world would come to know the living God. But as the story progresses we shall see what a costly thing it is to be a priesthood for all the nations.

Judges, kings and prophets

MOSES is on Mount Sinai and Israel is at the foot of the mountain, already forgetting their covenant and falling into paganism and idolatry. Moses has to wrestle with a disobedient and unbelieving Israel all through their journey across the desert. They must learn to depend on daily manna for food and miraculous springs from the rock for drink, and for their guidance a pillar of cloud by day and fire by night. Later generations would look back on those years as a time when Israel was taught to live by faith and not to seek any other kind of security.

BUT when Israel finally comes to the borders of the Promised Land, once again their faith fails them. The spies they sent out, with two exceptions, report that the inhabitants were too strong for them and the Israelites lose their courage and want to turn back again to Egypt. Once again God's patience seems to be exhausted, but Moses, the good priest of the priestly people, pleads with God for his people and God relents to the extent that their children at least shall come into the Promised Land.

REACHING THE PROMISED LAND

And so it was that a generation later, under Joshua, they crossed the Jordan, took possession of the land and expelled or slaughtered its native inhabitants. When we read this and compare it, for example, with the teaching of Jesus we are horrified by what we would now call ethnic cleansing. We have to remember that we are here dealing with the long, long story of the training of a people to understand the nature and purpose of God, and we are at an early stage in this training. We have to understand all of this in the light of the later teaching of Jesus.

The point here is that there was needed the 'experiment' of a people possessing a land in which the will of God could be expressed in a stable political, economic and social order – the kind of order indicated in the law books of the Pentateuch (Genesis to Deuteronomy). We can still learn from these what it would mean to have a society governed by the law of God. And although this was not to be in the case of Israel it nevertheless represents an essential part in the story of God's training of a people to be the priests for all the nations.

The book of Joshua gives us a picture of a complete settlement of the land, but when we move to the book of Judges we have a very different picture. All is not settled; there is chaos. Over and over again the people lapse into idolatry, are overrun by neighbouring nations, plead for help and are rescued by some kind of charismatic leader. There is mayhem, murder, gang rape and all kinds of horror. Over and over again there is the refrain:

At that time there was no king in Israel; everyone did what was right in his own eyes.

A picture of anarchy. And so the point comes at which the people begin to say, 'We want a king like the other nations'.

PROPHECY – THE NATION'S CONSCIENCE

And here we come to the beginning of the story of the prophets, who from Samuel to John the Baptist were to be the guides, warning, teaching, directing the people of Israel through the ensuing centuries. In this situation of chaos, when Israel is at the mercy of her neighbouring nations, when the priesthood is discredited and there is no stable rule, the people come to Samuel and say 'Give us a king'. And God tells Samuel to tell the people what it will be like to have a king: he will take their lands to be his gardens; he will take their women to be his concubines; he will take their men to be his soldiers and his forced labourers and his slaves; he will take their money in taxes. That is what a king will be like. But nevertheless the people say, 'We want a king, we want to be like the other nations.' They are tired of chaos. And God says to Samuel, 'Give them a king'. And Samuel anoints the young man Saul as king.

And so we have set out for the first time a theme which will appear throughout the Bible: the ambivalence of the political order. If we were all obedient to God's law we would not need a king, we would do from our hearts what is right. If we need kings, law courts, police and prisons it is because we have forsaken God. And therefore God gives us a political order, and yet he warns us that it is itself a source of profound corruption. That warning is sadly and swiftly realized. The kingship of Saul begins with such promise but ends in tragedy. Saul, tempted to insane jealousy of his ablest military leader, finally ends in the tragic suicide on Mount Gilboa and the defeat of Israel's armies.

There follows a period of confusion until David emerges as the leader of the whole nation of twelve tribes. And subsequent generations will look back on David's reign as an ideal time when true kingship was exercised in the maintenance of justice and the protection of the poor. And yet the Bible is quite frank in recording not only David's personal sin but also the confusion in his family life which was to lead to civil war and the sad ending of his kingdom.

David is followed by Solomon in whom the prophecies of Samuel are amply fulfilled. Solomon becomes a typical oriental potentate gathering to himself power, riches, women, gold, engaging in huge building projects and centralizing power in Jerusalem. It is not long, indeed Solomon is hardly in his grave, before the whole thing has broken up and his ablest labour leader, Jeroboam, has carried away ten of the twelve tribes to found a separate kingdom with Samaria as its capital, and to form a separate centre of worship to replace the temple in Jerusalem.

The centuries which follow tell us a miserable

story of wars between these two kingdoms – the northern kingdom of Israel and the smaller southern kingdom of Judah – and between these kingdoms and their neighbours – Philistia, Moab, Edom, Syria – while gradually the imperial power of Assyria dominates the eastern sky. The time comes when Assyria, after gobbling up all these small kingdoms, finally moves in to besiege and destroy Israel, take away its king, destroy the city of Samaria, remove its inhabitants to be slaves in the imperial estates of Assyria. In their place, pagan peoples from the east are moved in to colonize the land. The northern kingdom of Israel is ended.

Meanwhile the southern kingdom of Judah with its capital in Jerusalem was to hold out for some time longer. It had good kings and bad ones. The good king Hezekiah sought to restore the people to obedience to the law; the very bad king Manasseh did his best to destroy everything that Hezekiah had achieved. The good king Josiah sought (sadly too late) to bring Judah back to its true allegiance. In his time the version of the law which we find in the book of Deuteronomy was republished. And yet Judah too was doomed. The Assyrian empire had been replaced by Babylon as the superpower of the east, and in due course the Babylonian power was to reach into Judah. At first the city of Jerusalem was besieged and captured, its leaders removed and a puppet king installed and then, twelve years later, the city was finally destroyed, along with the temple, and all but a miserable remnant were taken into exile to be slaves and refugees in Babylon.

It looks as if this is the end of the story, as if God's promises to Abraham and to Moses have come to nothing. That it is not the end is due to the ministry of the great line of prophets from both the northern and the southern kingdoms: Elijah, Elisha, Amos, Hosea and others in the north; Isaiah, Micah and others in the south. These were raised up by God in generation after generation to warn Israel and Judah of the consequences of their folly; to remind the people of God's covenant of mercy and justice; to make clear to them that the God of Abraham, Isaac and Jacob is not like the gods of the nations, existing merely to sponsor the interests of that nation and satisfied as long as the necessary sacrifices and offerings are made.

The living God is a God of justice and mercy and he will be satisfied with nothing less than a people in whom his justice and his mercy are alive.

That message in generation after generation meant that the prophets had to speak against the spirit of their times, against popular opinion, against all the political powers – and to bear the consequences. Those who were faithful to this prophetic tradition were able to interpret the disasters which befall God's people not as a defeat for God but as the manifestation of God's righteous judgement. They were able to learn the hard lesson that to be God's chosen people meant to bear the sin of the world. They were able to point the way forward to that final consummation of the whole story in which the very son of God himself should suffer for the sin of the world.

Return and renewal

WE have reached what looks like a dead end. The two Israelite kingdoms of Israel and Judah have been destroyed. Their cities are in ruins, their people have been carried away captive and their temple has been burned to the ground. It looks as if the end of the line has come.

WHAT has become of the great promises to Abraham, Isaac and Jacob? What has become of the covenant with Moses? Of the promise that Israel is to be a royal priesthood, a holy nation on behalf of all the nations of the world? Can't we hear the mocking voice of the Gentiles as we listen to it in the psalms: 'Where is that God of yours now?' And is it not remarkable that in the same psalms we still hear, out of the depths of humiliation and suffering, this triumphant cry: 'Our God reigns and shall reign over all the nations'.

On any ordinary expectation one would have thought that this story would have been forgotten, buried in the rubble of history, unless perhaps it was dug up by modern archaeologists. How is it that this was not the end? The answer is in the work of those prophets to whom I have already referred – and very specially to two prophets living at the same time, one in Jerusalem and the other among the captive slaves in Babylon.

JEREMIAH AND EZEKIEL

The first of these, Jeremiah of Jerusalem, is one who perhaps more than any other mirrors in his life the ministry of Jesus. Jeremiah speaks of himself as a child who does not know how to speak and yet in the power of God he becomes a mighty fortress, standing for the truth amid all the storms and the violent and swirling currents of history in his time. He is absolutely clear that God's judgement is pronounced against his people. The reforms of Josiah have come too late. The people are too deeply corrupted. They still imagine that God is like one of the so-called gods of the nations, one whose only business is to protect them and look after their interests provided they offer all the necessary sacrifices and worship.

And so Jeremiah stands in the gate of the

temple while the crowds of worshippers stream in and says to them:

> 'It's no use. It's no use. It's no good saying "The temple of the Lord, the temple of the Lord, the temple of the Lord" (Jeremiah 7.4), and thinking that because you worship in this temple that God is going to protect you. He is not. He is going to punish you for all your sins.'

No wonder they put him in prison. And even when the armies of Babylon had captured the city and carried away its king and all its leading people and put a puppet king in his place, and Jeremiah was in prison, he still continued to affirm both God's judgement on the city and his absolutely unshakeable faith that in the end God would fulfil his promises and that he would rule again over his beloved land.

Meanwhile at the same time, another great prophet, Ezekiel, was giving to his fellow exiles in Babylon a matchless picture of the transcendent glory of God. Ezekiel convinced the people that God was still the Lord of all history, promising them a day when the mighty spirit of God would visit them afresh so that even a valley of dry bones could be turned into a mighty army, and assuring them that the glory of God would one day fill the temple in Jerusalem once again – and fill the whole world.

It was through the ministry of these great God-inspired prophets that the defeat and exile of Israel was to be interpreted: not as a defeat for God but as a manifestation of God's faithfulness to his covenant. It was under their inspiration that during these years of exile Jewish scribes and teachers brought together the ancient records of the earlier days of the Exodus and of the judges and the kings, and wrote those marvellous passages about the creation of the world.

It was through this experience that Israel was able to understand in a new way what it meant to be a holy nation. And it is from this time that we have the vision of Israel as the suffering servant of the Lord, who fulfils the Lord's will not by winning military victories but by bearing the sin of the world – the servant who will be numbered among the transgressors, upon whom the iniquity of us all will be laid. It was to these pictures that Jesus would turn for the interpretation of his own ministry and the true interpretation of Israel's calling.

POLITICS, POWER AND GOD'S PEOPLE

But meanwhile with the ever-changing ebb and flow of national politics, the power of Babylon is now replaced by that of Persia. And the newly reigning emperor Cyrus issues a decree that priests, Levites and other leaders may return to Jerusalem and rebuild the temple. God has been faithful: Cyrus is the instrument of God's gracious purpose to fulfil his promise to his covenant people. They have learnt that their exile and defeat is God's punishment for their sins. But now they have been punished enough. God's word to them is a word of comfort. They are to be forgiven, and they will return with joy and singing to Zion.

And so the Jewish leaders are able once again to re-establish a visible community even though it is not an autonomous state. The temple is rebuilt. The walls of Jerusalem are reconstructed under Nehemiah and the covenant renewed under the leadership of Ezra. And now there is yet another turn in the wheel of fortune. The empire of Persia is overrun by a still mightier empire, that of Greece. Alexander the Great sweeps through all the lands of the Middle East as far as India and establishes a new empire in which Greek language and Greek civilization are to replace the native cultures and religions of the area.

Greece prided itself on its unique civilization, its art, its philosophy, its religion – and the consequence of Alexander's victory was that the sacred places of Israel were desecrated. Greek culture was introduced: such phenomena as the Greek games with their naked athletics and Greek customs abhorrent to the Jews, such as the encouragement of homosexual practice, threatened this new kingdom with destruction.

Under the leadership of the family of the Maccabees a military revolt took place and in the ensuing wars thousands of faithful Israelites died rather than break God's commandments by fighting on the sabbath. Jerusalem was besieged and captured, and the leadership had to flee to the mountains in order to regroup and find a new base for their national life, an action which was to be echoed in later words of Jesus.

And from this time we have the great prophecy of Daniel with his vision of the brutal beast-like empires of Assyria and Babylon, Persia and Greece, each trampling the earth with their mighty powers. But there comes to the Ancient of Days one not like a beast but like a son of man and to him is given the power to reign and of his kingdom there shall be no end. And the question always was, 'When will this son of man appear?'

But always there was a faithful remnant in Israel. It now had a new source of strength. The action of Israel's scribes in the period of exile in bringing together the written records of Israel's history to form the books of the law and the prophets provided the basis for a new kind of religious life. Certainly the sacrificial worship of the temple in Jerusalem still continued. But a new and vital centre of religious life was developed in the synagogue where God was worshipped in the singing of the psalms, in the reading of the law and the prophets, and in prayer for the coming of God's kingdom.

Israel was again a visible community. And yet how small, how feeble! What a puny thing the temple was compared to the mighty temple of Solomon. In the psalms we hear the voice of this faithful remnant. On the one hand there is the mocking word of the Gentiles who had lordship over them:

'Where is now this God of yours who rescued you out of Egypt?'

But on the other hand there is both the triumphant cry:

'God reigns over all the nations'

– and that cry from the depths of humiliation and darkness:

'O Lord, how long, how long?'

And we come to the last three books of the Old Testament, Zechariah, Haggai and Malachi, which hold out the promise that the messenger of the Lord will come and establish his reign. It is to these three books that Jesus most frequently appeals in his later teaching. But meanwhile, in one more turn of the political wheel, the power of Greece was to be overcome by the still greater power of Rome. Israel becomes a province of the Roman Empire. The Holy Land is trampled by the feet of Roman soldiers and the people of Israel have to acknowledge another lordship than that of God by paying taxes to the emperor in Rome. And still the cry goes up, 'How long?'

It is into this world that Jesus will be born.

God's kingdom and Jesus

IN our journey through the story told in the Bible we have come to the time when Jesus is to be born.

THE children of Israel no longer inhabit their own kingdom. They are scattered right across the Mediterranean world and far into what we now call the Middle East. They are without their own king or their own kingdom. Assyria, Babylon, Persia and Greece have all gone, but the mighty power of Rome still dominates the world, and Israel still longs for the day when they will see the fulfilment of God's promise that he will reign over all the nations. And there is a faithful remnant in the land which continues to cry out in the words of the psalms:

'Lord, how long?'

The faithful remnant is centred in the worship of the synagogue with its reading of the law and the prophets and its singing of the psalms, always looking towards that day when God's reign will be manifest. The puppet king Herod, installed by the Roman power, has rebuilt the temple on a magnificent scale, hoping thereby to ingratiate himself with the people, and the temple worship is carried on. But the synagogues are the main centre of devout hope and faith. One may say that there were four different ways in which this hope for the kingdom was expressed.

1. POLITICAL REVOLT

There were in the first place those who thought that the Maccabees had given the right example – that Israel must rise in revolt and throw out the pagan power. And so there was always an eager expectation of some leader who would arise and rally Israel to the cause as the Maccabees had done. And there was a continual succession of such freedom fighters, all of whose revolts were ruthlessly crushed by the Roman power so that the sight of a crucified terrorist hanging from a cross by the wayside had become terribly familiar to the people of Israel.

2. CO-OPERATION

At the other end of the spectrum were the

priests and the Sadducees who administered Herod's temple and who had made a kind of accommodation with the ruling power. They too looked for the coming of the kingdom of God, but for the time being they were content to work alongside the ruling powers and to continue the worship of the temple as laid down in the law.

3. KEEPING THE LAW

And then there were the Pharisees, whose worship and life were centred in the synagogues, with their regular reading of the law and the prophets. It was their faith that if Israel could perfectly keep God's law, then God would in his own way and time intervene to establish his kingdom. And they therefore sought to ensure the meticulous and absolute obedience of all true Israelites to the law in all its detail.

4. WITHDRAWAL

Finally there were those who had withdrawn from public life, those about whom we know through the recently discovered Dead Sea scrolls. They had established monastic communities in the desert, withdrawing from the conflicts of public life, believing that by a regime of prayer and fasting they could hasten the day when God would intervene to save his people and establish his reign.

THE WAY OF JESUS

It is into this world that Jesus was born. We know very little about the first thirty years of his life except for that fascinating glimpse of him as a child of twelve in the temple, discussing the interpretation of Scripture with the teachers of the law. But there are two things I think we can confidently say on the basis of what we know from his later teaching.

First we can be confident that he was a master of the Scriptures, as already suggested by that story of his childhood visit to the temple. We can affirm this because of the fact that even his enemies addressed him as 'rabbi'. The word rabbi did not denote, as it does now, a professional teacher. It was given to anyone who showed himself to be a true master of the interpretation of Scripture. The fact that Jesus was consistently addressed as rabbi even by his opponents shows that he was indeed acknowledged to be such a master, and we must take it that in those hidden years before his public ministry he was deeply engaged in the search to hear his father's word in the Scriptures.

The second thing that we can confidently say is that from the beginning Jesus knew God as his father. We can say this because of the word that he consistently used in addressing God, the word *abba*. This is a Aramaic word expressing the deepest possible intimacy between a child and its father. The Gospels, as we know, were written in Greek, the public language of the time. Why then do the writers go out of the way to keep this Aramaic word? Surely it was because they could never forget the actual sound of this word on the lips of Jesus. It was the word that characteristically expressed his relationship to his father. And we can affirm, I think confidently, that in those hidden years, Jesus was both engaged in the profound study of the Scriptures and that he knew God as his father in the most intimate possible way.

But meanwhile Israel waited for God to act. It seemed that there was a long, long silence. It was centuries since the authentic voice of prophecy had been heard in the land. But there came a day when the rumour reached the streets and bazaars of Nazareth of a new prophet, John, Jesus' kinsman, who had appeared in the desert and who seemed to represent once again the authentic figure and voice of a prophet like Elijah. And his was a radical call to the whole of Israel to repent.

Israel had entered the Promised Land by going through the waters of Jordan. John calls Israel to go back to the starting point, to make a radically fresh beginning, to go through the waters of Jordan in a baptism of repentance for the forgiveness of sins and to make a new start. And multitudes were responding to this call. To Jesus this came as a call from his father. He knew that his hour had come, and a day came when he laid down the carpenter's tools for the last time and took the long road down from the hills of Galilee to the banks of the Jordan. We see him in public for the first time, standing among a crowd of repentant sinners asking for the baptism of repentance for the forgiveness of sins. He makes no distinction between himself and them. He is part of Israel. He is identified with Israel in its sin. He is numbered with the transgressors. John, as we know, resisted, but Jesus insisted and so went down into the waters of the Jordan and received from John the baptism of repentance for the forgiveness of sins.

And then that event happened which was to

launch Jesus on his public ministry. He heard a voice from heaven:

'This is my beloved son in whom I am well pleased.'

And he received from heaven that anointing of the Holy Spirit which Ezekiel and the prophets had promised: the Holy Spirit of power to bring in the kingly reign of God. And that is why from the time of Jesus onwards we have to rethink the very concept of God in terms of Father, Son and Holy Spirit.

Immediately, in the power of the spirit, Jesus is driven out into the desert to face the awesome question, 'What does it mean to be the son of God? What does it mean to be anointed by the spirit to usher in God's kingdom?' And for those forty days Jesus wrestled in the wilderness, facing one after another of the choices which the world offers for winning leadership among men and women. There is first of all the economic route: satisfy their immediate needs, feed the hungry, give them what they need. Give them the feel-good factor and they will follow you. Jesus rejects that.

And there is the religious way: do something

spectacular, something which cannot be explained except as a miraculous act of God and the people will follow you. Jesus rejects that.

And there is the political route: mobilize the political forces of the world in order to gain control over the world. Jesus could have taken that route, but he rejected it and in rejecting it we can say that he chose the way of the cross. And so he comes back from the desert, back to his native Galilee and makes this great ringing announcement:

'The time has come. The kingdom of God is at hand. Repent and believe and follow me.'

'Well, what is new? Every devout Jew knows that God reigns! It's what he sings in the temple every sabbath. So what's new?'

'What is new is that the kingdom of God is here now, facing you.'

'But where is it? We don't see it!'

'You don't see it because you are looking the wrong way. You are expecting something different. Turn round, repent and come with me. Believe me and come with me and you will discover what the kingdom of God is.'

Because the truth is that Jesus himself is the presence of the kingdom. The kingdom is not a new political regime. It is not a new programme. It is not a new ideology. It is not a new philosophy. It is the person of Jesus. And to know what God's kingly rule is, one must believe in Jesus and come with him.

Well this sets the whole of Galilee tingling with excitement. People follow him, but people are also perplexed: 'What is this kingdom? Where is the kingdom?' They follow but they question, and they are puzzled.

And in the next chapter we will try to show how Jesus taught and manifested the reign of God in his own ministry.

Sacrifice

WE have arrived at the point where Jesus has come into Galilee announcing that the kingdom of God has come.

MOST of Jesus' hearers thought it was quite clear: God is the rightful king of all the earth and all these rulers – Assyria, Babylon, Persia, Greece, Rome – are all usurpers. To say that the kingdom of God is at hand must mean that the Roman power is about to be thrown out and that Israel is going to be once again under the direct rule of God, who from Zion will rule all the nations. So naturally when Jesus announces that the kingdom of God is at hand it creates immense excitement. There are crowds who come to listen but there is also scepticism, there is puzzlement. What exactly does this kingdom mean?

Naturally also the authorities in Jerusalem are worried, and so they send scouts to find out what is going on, to listen to Jesus and discover whether in fact he is really a trouble maker.

And so Jesus has to use coded language in his teaching, he speaks in parables so that the scouts from Jerusalem cannot pick up his words and use them as a basis for an arrest. But on the other hand those with ears to hear will be able to understand.

But it is not only words. Jesus has an extra-ordinary authority. With a word he heals the sick; he gives sight to the blind; he cleanses the lepers. And what is even more serious, he announces the forgiveness of sins. The law provides a proper procedure for the forgiveness of sins: one goes to the temple and offers the necessary sacrifices and through the mediation of the priest one receives forgiveness. Jesus has come to set people free. His words have an extraordinary authority. They have power. And yet they are words of grace and kindness. But at the same time they are words as sharp as a razor.

Out of the crowds who followed, some friendly, some curious and some hostile, Jesus had chosen twelve to be his special companions so that by living with him, sharing in all his wanderings, in his teachings, in his meals, they would learn to know him in his own full reality as the presence of the kingdom of God. They were of course also exposed to all the ideas that were floating

58

around among the general public about who Jesus was.

A NEW KIND OF KINGDOM

Jesus takes his close companions to a place away from the crowds and puts to them a question:

'Who do you believe that I am?'

And God puts it into the heart of Simon Peter to give that decisive answer:

'You are the Christ, you are the one whom God has sent to reign, to establish his kingdom.'

And immediately Jesus begins to teach them what kind of a kingship this will be. In line with all that he had learned from the Scriptures he taught them that the one who reigns in God's name must be one who suffers, who is rejected, who is humiliated but who will finally be vindicated. And in order that this might be strengthened in the minds of his disciples, God gave to him and to them that marvellous experience on the Mount of Transfiguration when

Jesus was filled with the glory of God and the disciples had a vision of Moses and Elijah – representing the law and the prophets – bearing witness to Jesus and encouraging him on his way to the cross. And from that moment Jesus sets his face to go to Jerusalem for the final showdown.

He chooses for his final entry the season of the Passover, that season of maximum excitement, maximum expectation that God would deliver his people once again as he had delivered them from Egypt in those events which are commemorated at Passover time. And he chooses as the manner of his final showdown a prophecy from Zechariah which spoke of a king who would come riding on a donkey to claim his kingship.

So Jesus rode on a donkey, accompanied by his disciples and his followers, right into Jerusalem and right into the heart of the temple. And there he threw out those who were doing the necessary business of the temple – namely providing the animals for sacrifice and the special coinage for the official offerings, thus for one symbolic day bringing to a halt the regular worship of the temple. Why did he do this? As his teaching made clear it was to demonstrate that God's judgement had been pronounced upon this temple, that it would be destroyed and that in its place there would be a new temple, a new place where God dwells, a new place where sacrifice can be offered and where men and women can know that they are in the home of God. That temple would be built not with the gigantic stones of Herod's temple but with the living stones of men and women reconciled to God through Jesus Christ.

It was the most open possible challenge to the leadership of Israel and it could not go unanswered. For obvious reasons Jesus did not stay in Jerusalem during those days leading up to the Passover but spent the nights in a nearby village. But each day of the following week he sat in the temple openly teaching, with no further need for concealment. And among the parables of that week was one of which the meaning could not possibly be doubted. Jesus took the old parable from Isaiah, which spoke of Israel as God's vineyard in which he hoped to grow the fruit of justice and mercy but in which he had failed to find fruit. Jesus retells that story with the owner of the vineyard sending his messengers one after another, all of them to be rejected by the tenants, until finally the owner of the vineyard plays his last card and sends his beloved son. And him they cast out and kill.

No one could possibly doubt the meaning of that parable: the authorities must either surrender to the teaching of Jesus or destroy him. And the decision is taken to destroy him. But it was necessary that his disciples should be prepared to face what was to come. And so on the last day before the Passover he gathered his disciples together for one of their familiar meals and demonstrated in an action something that words alone could never show. He took the bread of their meal, broke it, gave it to them and said:

'This is my body broken for you.'

He took a cup, shared it with them, and said:

'This is the new covenant in my blood shed for you and for many. Drink it all of you.'

What do these actions mean? Their meaning is surely plain. He is saying to them, 'What I now have to do I must do alone'. No one else can do what Jesus has to do at that moment. But he is doing it not in order that they may be left behind, but in order that they may follow, that they may be with him, that they may be actual partakers in his act of final sacrifice. This cup will be the new covenant which Jeremiah had promised, in which the law of God will be written not on tablets of stone but in the hearts of men and women. And he commands them to do this so that when everything else seems to have been shattered beyond repair, they will have this action to bind them forever to him and make them partakers of his dying and of his victory.

DEATH AND VICTORY

And so he leads them down that long flight of steps – which is still there today – into the garden of Gethsemane. There is that final agony of doubt, 'Is this indeed the father's will?' And Jesus in that final agony masters all the doubts and temptations that could assail him and surrenders himself to his father's will. And when he goes up those steps again it is without the disciples for they have panicked and fled. It is as a prisoner to be tried and condemned.

So he comes face to face with those who have become unwittingly the agents of the enemy –

Caiaphas and Pilate. And when challenged he bears witness to the fact that he is indeed that son of man whose coming had been promised. And so he is condemned, humiliated, flogged, taken out to die. One more crucified fighter for the kingdom. But unlike all who had gone before, Jesus' words are not curses for those who torture him, but words of forgiveness. As each nail is hammered in he repeats the words 'Father forgive them', and his final words are of peace and forgiveness to a terrorist crucified beside him, and for his heartbroken mother and disciple.

Then come those terrible hours of darkness, followed by the cry:

'My God, why hast thou forsaken me?'

At the very beginning of this book I referred to the cry of God in the garden of Eden:

'Adam, where are you?'

The agonized father seeking for the son who has been lost. Now the beloved son of the father has shared the fate of the lost children, and with them, for them, on their behalf, as one of them, he cries out to the father:

64

'My God, why hast thou forsaken me?'

He goes down into the very depths of dereliction so that there could be no depths of despair into which we could ever fall in which the son of God would not be there beside us. And then all things achieved he cries out:

'It is finished.'

The work is done. The prince of this world is cast out. And Jesus bows his head and gives up his spirit. This is the victory that overcomes the world – how it is, and how it has been seen to be, will be the subject of our next chapter.

New life, new communities

SO Jesus has been crucified, is dead and has been buried. To his contemporaries it must have seemed that this was just one more failed revolution, one more nail in the coffin of Jewish hopes for the kingdom of God.

How has it happened that today, among all the world's faith communities, much the largest and still rapidly growing is that community which looks to the cross as the sign of victory? The one way in which it can be explained is the story told in the Bible itself, namely that on the third day the tomb in which Jesus had been laid was empty and that he was rallying his disciples and sending them out as his witnesses into all the world.

LIFE AFTER DEATH

Here we come to the crunch issue. It is not difficult to believe in a good man who was condemned and put to death. But that three days later he was alive and radiant and inspiring his disciples to a new worldwide mission? That runs against everything in our experience. If it is true it requires a radical rethinking of everything we have understood hitherto about the fundamental nature of the world. And this is not a new problem. It is rather silly to suggest that it arises because of our modern scientific knowledge. The fact that people who have been dead for three days don't rise again on the third day was well known long before the invention of computers. No! The Church has always recognized that this is something utterly unique, something which cannot be explained in terms of the ordinary laws of physics and chemistry.

But there is one analogy for it, one other fact which cannot be explained by the laws of physics and chemistry and biology – and that is the fact of creation, the fact that a world has come into existence. And the Christian Church has always maintained that what happened on that Easter day was a kind of new creation, the beginning of a new era for the world. The first fruit of God's intention to recreate the whole cosmos according to his glorious purpose. That I believe is the truth. I do not believe that on any other basis one can make sense of the subsequent history.

And so we now continue the story on the basis of this biblical record.

How marvellously this astounding news is broken. How gently this explosion of new reality breaks on the world. The women who alone seem not to have been totally shattered by the events of Good Friday come to the tomb, they have a vision, they are told he is alive but they don't believe it. Mary Magdalene, the first to whom the risen Lord appears, runs to tell the disciples – but they do not believe. And yet slowly bit by bit there are more and more evidences, more and more stories that make it impossible to doubt that he is indeed alive. And finally Jesus rallies his disciples, sends them out to proclaim what the world must know: that death, sin, the devil have been finally conquered and that Jesus is the Lord of all. Because the world must know who is in charge, to whom all men and women are ultimately responsible. Everyone must know – we have no right to keep that secret to ourselves. And so the news spreads. First of all among Jews, because the ministry of Jesus was first of all to Israel.

Jesus has told his disciples that they are to wait in Jerusalem because they will receive that full anointing by the Holy Spirit which had been

71

promised in the prophets and which he had received at his baptism. And so with joy and expectation they wait in Jerusalem until the day comes when they do indeed receive that anointing of power which sets them alight and drives them out into the streets tingling with the joy of this new message.

Conflict and unity

There is rejection but there is also acceptance, and so there is inevitably conflict. The news spreads first among the Jews and then among the Gentiles. We come to the remarkable ministry of Saul (later known as Paul) who had been a leader in the persecution of the early Church, but who was confronted on the road to Damascus by the living Lord Jesus and turned into a blazing apostle of the new faith. He and his colleague Barnabas worked in Antioch helping to develop a great new community of people – both Jews and Gentiles – who knew that Jesus was Lord. This was a new phenomenon. Every Jew knows that the world is divided into Jews and Gentiles. But if Gentiles accept Jesus as Lord and are baptized into the family of Jesus, what are they? They are no longer heathen. They are not

Jews by race – but they are not Gentiles either. There had to be a new name to give to this new reality. I imagine in India that we might have called them 'Messiahwallas'. The name they gave them in Antioch was 'Christians'. And Christians became a community that spread throughout the world, especially as the apostles went from city to city throughout the whole of what we now call the Middle and Near East. Remember that in all the great cities of the Mediterranean world there were synagogues where the scattered Jewish community met on the sabbath to read the law and the prophets and to pray for the coming of the kingdom. And around these synagogues there was always a company of Gentiles who were attracted by the purity of the Jewish faith and were spoken of as 'godfearers'.

When Paul and the other apostles went around the synagogues and were invited as visiting scholars to give whatever message they had, they stood up to announce that what had been read in the law and the prophets in the earlier part of the service had now been fulfilled in the coming of Jesus. Those wonderful pictures of the suffering servant, the servant of the Lord upon whom the sin of the world is laid and who bears all our transgressions – they have been fulfilled in the life and ministry and death and resurrection of Jesus.

Inevitably this again created conflict. There were those who accepted this news with joy. But there were those who could not accept it. And so the division arose between the two groups, and more and more Christians separated themselves from those who could not accept this message and who must therefore continue to hope that God's promises would finally be fulfilled in a new age in which Zion would become the capital of the world and Jehovah would rule all the nations.

NEW AND OLD

In the book of the Acts of the Apostles we get a picture of the Church moving westwards until finally it is established in the centre of the empire in Rome, in the person of Paul who is there as an apostle but also as a prisoner, awaiting death in the footsteps of his master. And in the great epistles which form the next part of the New Testament we have windows into the inner life of that young Church and the problems it had to face.

The great problem was how to relate the new message of the gospel to the old law. Were all the laws of Moses binding upon the Gentiles? Could Gentiles who became Christians continue to behave in the way that Gentiles had done in the past? Ways which were an abomination in the eyes of Israel? Crucial was the question of circumcision which had always been foundational in Jewish practice. Paul's answer to this problem was that circumcision had been given to Abraham and his successors as a sign and not as a precondition of the grace of God, that the promises of God came before the law of God and that what was a sign must not be turned into a condition.

In the greatest of his letters – the letter to the Romans – Paul is looking forward to the time when, having finished his ministry in the eastern part of the Mediterranean, he hopes to move to the west and make Rome the centre of a new mission to the whole western Mediterranean. There is already in Rome a church consisting of Jewish and Gentile converts and he wants them to understand his message and to grasp the way in which he sees the relation between the old and the new. There are also letters – for example to the Corinthians – which deal with quite different problems. How are Gentiles to act under their new lordship of Jesus Christ? How are Gentiles, born and brought up as Gentiles and living still in a wholly Gentile environment – how are they to obey the law of God as it is set forth in Jesus?

And in the epistle to the Hebrews, there is a parallel to Paul's argument about how Jesus fulfils the moral law. The writer of this letter shows that Jesus also fulfils all that is written in the Old Testament concerning the priestly ministry of the temple and the priesthood – that in Jesus, all that was prescribed in the Old Testament by way of offering, sacrifice and priesthood has been fulfilled so that the Christian Church is itself now in Christ a holy priesthood.

The New Testament continues with the pastoral letters of Peter, James and John, which give us a picture of how these new communities of Christians are to order their lives so that they can become centres of new life in the midst of that dying Roman world. And finally we come to the book of the Revelation of St John in which the final consummation of all things is prefigured – and that will be the theme of the last chapter in this book.

Future revelation

WE are coming to the end of this story of the Bible as a whole – a story which focuses on the particular history of one nation, Israel, and focuses on one man, Jesus. And so the story is told because God has chosen Israel and Jesus to be bearers of his purpose for the whole of creation and of the human race.

AT the beginning of the Bible, before we begin to have the story of Israel beginning with Abraham, we have those first eleven chapters of Genesis which speak of the creation of the world. And now at the end of the Bible we have the book called the Revelation of St John, a picture of the end of the world. We ended the last chapter with St Paul in Rome, the centre of the civilized world as it knew itself – Paul as a missionary but also as a martyr, facing death for his master's sake.

In the story told in the Gospels Rome is in the background. Now Rome moves to the centre.

Rome, that mighty power which dominated the known world with its awesome military strength, its vast commercial networks stretching right across the known world, its propaganda machine constantly saturating the world with its own ideology of power and glory; Rome which in its own eyes was the apex of human civilization, but which in the eyes of Israel was the great harlot seducing the world with false claims to glory. And in this final book of the Bible we see the ultimate resolution of the conflict between God and this centre of power – a conflict in which all that is opposed to God has its most concentrated expression. And the conflict will be fought out between this power on the one hand and the one who is described in this book as the 'Lion of Judah' and the 'Lamb slain from the foundation of the world'. From one side it will be fought with all the weapons of military, commercial and ideological power. On the other side it will be fought with the weapons of faith, hope and patient suffering and sacrifice.

On the one side there is the power of the lie – untruths which are multiplied many times through all the machinery of propaganda. On the other side there is the word of truth, spoken and acted in Jesus, the word which is like a sharp two-edged sword, cutting through all the subterfuges, confusions and lies that fill the world. And this means that in the end there must be a day of judgement. As Jesus had said:

'There is nothing hidden that will not be revealed.'

In the end there will be no space for delusion. Everything will be seen as it is. That is the meaning of Jesus being the light of the world: it means that in his presence there can be no lies. Everything must be seen as it truly is.

Rome represents, from the point of view of the Bible, the supreme example of what had been exemplified in Babylon, Assyria, Persia and Greece – the pride of humankind seeking to establish in our own power the final authority over the human race. God's response to this is the gift of the holy city which is not the achievement of human power but the gift of God's grace, perfect in beauty, embodying all the perfection to which human culture in all its forms aspires – its politics, its culture, its art and everything that we summarize in the word 'civilization'. Into that city we are told that the kings of the earth shall bring their treasures. In that sense it is the consummation of the whole human struggle to create a truly good and beautiful world. But it will not be the product of human pride; it will be the gift of God.

HISTORY AND OUR STORY

At the beginning of this book I said that the Bible gives us the whole story of creation and of the human race and therefore enables us to understand our own lives as part of that story. But every human attempt to see the story as a whole runs into an insuperable difficulty. If the meaning of my life is its contribution to some historical project of civilization which in the end will lead to a perfect society in the future, then from my point of view the problem is that I shall not be there to share in it. I shall be dead before it arrives. And that means that I am essentially expendable. I am not part of God's ultimate purpose. The logic of this has been developed with terrible precision in some of the movements of the twentieth century in which millions of men and women have been sacrificed for the sake of some ideology, some vision of a perfect society in the future.

If I cannot accept this, if I cannot believe that

my human life and the lives of those whom I know and love are simply raw material like the shavings left on a workshop floor after the job is done, then the alternative seems to be that I seek for meaning in personal fulfilment. And that inevitably takes me away in the end from total involvement in the human project of civilization. It means that I am led to put my hope in some personal future for myself which must necessarily be beyond this world because I shall not be present when this world comes to its goal. And so there is a kind of spirituality that leads us away from our active involvement in the business of this world. That is what my Indian friend meant (as quoted in chapter 1) when he said that the Bible was not a book of religion but was a unique interpretation of universal history and therefore an interpretation of the human person as a responsible actor in history.

So the alternatives seem to be either finding meaning for history as a whole at the cost of no meaning for my personal life; or else finding meaning for my personal life at the cost of no meaning for the story as a whole. To discover the third option – which I believe to be the answer – we have to recognize that the core of the problem is death. It is death that removes me from the story before it reaches its end. And death, as the Bible tells us, is the wages of sin. We die because nothing that we have done or been is good enough for God's perfect kingdom. I know that before my obituary is written. We are not fit for God's eternal kingdom. What the gospel does is to show us that Jesus' life from a purely earthly point of view ended in failure – and yet, because he committed himself in total obedience and love to his father, he was raised by the father to glory as the first fruits of a new creation.

So in so far as I commit all that I do, imperfect as it is, to God in Jesus Christ, knowing that much of it is utterly unfit to survive and yet trusting that what has been committed in faith will find its place in God's final kingdom, that gives me something to look forward to in which both my hopes for the world and my hopes for myself are brought together. The book of Revelation offers us the vision of a city which is on the one hand the perfection of all human striving towards beauty, civilization and good order, and on the other hand is the place where every tear is dried and where every one of us knows God face to face, and knows that we are his and he is ours. That is the vision with which the Bible ends, and it is a vision that enables us to see the whole human story and each of our lives within that story as meaningful, and which therefore invites us through Jesus Christ to become responsible actors in history, not to seek to run away from the responsibilities and the agonies of human life in its public dimension. Each of us must be ready to take our share in all the struggles and the anguish of human history and yet with the confidence that what is committed to Christ will in the end find its place in his final kingdom.

That means that as I look forward I don't see just an empty void, I don't just see my own death, I don't just see some future utopia in which I shall have no share. The horizon to which I look forward is that day when Jesus shall come, and his holy city will come down as a bride from heaven adorned for her husband.

The Society for Promoting Christian Knowledge (SPCK) was founded in 1698. It has as its purpose three main tasks:

- **Communicating the Christian faith in its rich diversity**

- **Helping people to understand the Christian faith and to develop their personal faith**

- **Equipping Christians for mission and ministry**

SPCK Worldwide serves the Church through Christian literature and communication projects in over 100 countries. Special schemes also provide books for those training for ministry in many parts of the developing world. SPCK Worldwide's ministry involves Churches of many traditions. This worldwide service depends upon the generosity of others and all gifts are spent wholly on ministry programmes, without deductions.

SPCK Bookshops support the life of the Christian community by making available a full range of Christian literature and other resources, and by providing support to bookstalls and book agents throughout the UK. SPCK Bookshops' mail order department meets the needs of overseas customers and those unable to have access to local bookshops.

SPCK Publishing produces Christian books and resources, covering a wide range of inspirational, pastoral, practical and academic subjects. Authors are drawn from many different Christian traditions, and publications aim to meet the needs of a wide variety of readers in the UK and throughout the world.

The Society does not necessarily endorse the individual views contained in its publications, but hopes they stimulate readers to think about and further develop their Christian faith.

For further information about the Society, please write to:
SPCK, Holy Trinity Church, Marylebone Road,
London NW1 4DU, United Kingdom.
Telephone: 020 7387 5282